*Signature of a Prophet*

# FRANCINA NORMAN

# *Signature of a Prophet*

Leave a Signature That Will Impact Generations to Come

# TABLE OF CONTENTS

# ACKNOWLEDGMENTS

I want to thank my husband Pastor Michael Norman who understood my value and challenged me to never put myself on clearance.

To my children Dirk, LaTau, and Brittney allowing me to grow as your mother. To my grandson Brice, your challenges in life have brought so much strength to our family while blessing us with your unconditional love. To Alicia, thank you for being a great mother to Brice. To Maxine, you have shown our family true Agape love as Brice's grandmother. To my Mom, the late Bessie Pinckney

A Signature was left by the generals and spiritual parents, who have gone on to be with the Lord, Bishop Isaiah Williams, Pastor Mary Perry, Bishop Milton Perry, Mother Ruth Crockett, Elaine Kimble, Dr. Myles and Ruth Munroe, Fuchsia Pickett and Pastor Stan Moore.

To my spiritual mom Dr. Gloria Williams, and Apostle Pam Vinnett defining my calling as as prophet. Pastor Agu and Sola Irukwu and Jesus House UK family for your love and support in the UK, Dr. Shola and Funke Adeaga my dear friends, Pastor Femi and Debora Atoyebi for believing in my ministry, Pastor Andrew and Yemi Adeleke of House of Praise UK for exposing me to RCCG, to RCCG Family domestic and abroad, Rev Funke and Bishop Felix Adejumo for exposing me to Nigeria, Bishop Gregory Foster hosting my first revival, Apostle Ed and Yvette Brinson, Pastor Randall & Felicity Cunningham, Alexis Snyder, Pastor Betty Brown, Her Excellence Rachael Ruto, my long time prayer partner Lady Servena Stevens.

To my co labors Apostle Sharaine Lathon, Prophet Cynthnia Thompson, Dr Michael and Samantha Phillips, Adaeze Okike providing a Safe House for my Healing.

To to a host of family and Friends,Who have impacted my life. Thank you. I want to thank my God for this amazing journey to impact the world and the opportunity God grace me The Signature of A Prophet.

# INTRODUCTION

## THE SIGNATURE

*What Is More Binding, Your Initials Or Your Signature?* When reading a legal document, your *INITIALS* demonstrate that you have viewed the contents of the page. However, *INITIALS* alone do not signify that you are agreeing to the terms of the document, it simply means you acknowledge that you are reviewed that page. Initials can show that someone has read or received something, but they do not have the same importance as a *SIGNATURE*.  A signature indicates that you not only have read the contents of the document, but that you are in agreement with the content and agree to be bound by it.  Your initials on a check or contract do not make it a binding agreement. Your SIGNATURE is required for it to be valid and binding.

In the same way, you have *SIGNATURES* in the Spirit.  There are many prophets that are leaving only their initials when they minister and it is not carrying the same weight, authority or impact as their God intended signature.  A *SIGNATURE* in the natural is a handwritten representation of all, or a substantial portion, of one's name.  It is a mark or sign made by an individual on a  document to signify knowledge, approval, acceptance or obligation.

The term signature is generally understood to mean the signing of a written document with one's own hand.  The purpose of a signature is to authenticate a writing or provide notice of its source.  It is also to bind the individual signing the document by the provisions contained in the document.

Our duty as prophets is to leave the full weight of our signature on the earth and to prepare our next generation to be authentic and bold for God.  When you look at the prophets of old, they were authentic. Their ministering carried weight and authority and left a notable, marked impact as a result.  On the contrary today, there are many prophets leaving only their initials, which are not representing the voice and authority of God.  Entertainment and imitation has replaced authenticity therefore causing a lack of real life change and significant impact as a result.

The goal of this book is for you to discover your authenticity and authority and for you to embrace it.  It is to enable you to hear God clearly so that you will be equipped to be a blessing to your local church and prepare the next generation to walk in that same boldness, authenticity and authority.  Nothing is binding until you leave your *SIGNATURE* on the earth.  As we come together with one mind and one heart to know and please God, our nations will experience "The Signature of a Prophet."  May you leave your *SIGNATURE* in the earth that will impact generations to come.

# CHAPTER 1
## THE PROPHET

*"Formerly in Israel, when a man went to inquire of God, he spoke thus: "Come, let us go to the seer"; for he who is now called a prophet was formerly called a seer."*

**1 Samuel 9:9**

In ancient Israel, the term "seer" was the title given a prophet as seen here in 1 Samuel 9:9. One of the most fundamental and basic abilities of a prophet is the ability to see in the spirit, beyond what the natural eyes can see. Every function of a prophet is based upon their ability to see, which is why a prophet is called a seer.

When the prophet Jeremiah was only a child, God began to reveal to him his identity as a prophet. God began to show Jeremiah varying visions and would ask him the simple question, "What do you *SEE?*" As Jeremiah would answer God as to what it was he was seeing by the Spirit, God would commend him on it and then show him what the things he was seeing signified. Every prophet must have the ability to see the visions of God. Every prophet is a seer. From this foundation of being able to see, there are several functions that a prophet operates in and is sent to earth to do for God.

In the New Testament, John the Baptist was a prophet. He served as a fore runner of Jesus Christ. When it was his time to begin to function as a prophet, he began to proclaim the message of God concerning the coming of the Kingdom of Heaven, which was referring to the coming of the Messiah Jesus Christ. One of the primary functions of a prophet is to be the forerunner's voice of the things to come.

*"For this is he who was spoken of by the prophet Isaiah, saying: "The voice of one crying in the wilderness: 'Prepare the way of the Lord; Make His paths straight."*

**MATTHEW 3:3**

A forerunner by definition is one who "goes before and announces the coming of another." It is also defined as one who "prepares and paves the way for the success and accomplishment of another." Prophets must clearly understand their role has a clearly defined, two-fold focus. The primary is to go before and announce the coming of the future things. The second one is to raise up others to achieve success and accomplishment in establishing God's Kingdom.

Forerunners not only make the announcements, but they also are to pave the way for the success and accomplishment of the things they proclaim. Therefore, being a forerunner is not a self-focused ministry. This is often very different that what is witnessed when considering some of the prophetic ministers of our generation. An authentic, truly SIGNATURE bearing prophetic ministry is one focused on declaring AND helping to establish the accomplishment and success of those God is sending in the coming season.

When prophets understand this role, remaining selfless and maintaining their focus on God's assignment is much easier. In addition, it is not until the prophet understands and accepts their role of selflessness and responsibility to make others a success that they will experience the full weight of authority to leave a SIGNATURE in the earth. God only releases the weight of spiritual authority to those He can trust to do what He has sent them to do. The degree the prophet can be trusted by God to be selfless and stay focused is the measure of the weight of the prophet's anointing.

Prophets are also stewards of the mysteries of God. A steward manages and distributes as directed the resource to which they are assigned. As a prophet you are assigned to the mysteries of God. Webster's dictionary defines a mystery as "a religious truth that one can know only by revelation and cannot fully understand." The truths, which are the principles and mind of God, are mysteries.

These mysteries are hidden in the Word of God, in the happenings of the world and universe around us and even in the dreams of people.

As a prophet, God entrusts you with these mysteries. He reveals to you as a seer, through revelation, what His principles are in these mysteries. In the Word of God, you will see principles that because of the revelation and insight He has given you, are plain to you, but not easily recognized by others. You will clearly see His mysteries in things that happen in the world and even in the universal atmosphere that are powerful revelations of His season and what is coming. In the dreams that people share with you, His great mysteries are often also revealed as He gives you the interpretation of those dreams.

The most important thing to understand is that, as a prophet, you are a *STEWARD* of these mysteries. You cannot and should not handle these mysteries as your own or distribute them according to your own will. You must share them and speak of them according to the desire of the One who gave you the stewardship over them.

When a prophet lacks understanding of their role as a steward, they are prone to using these mysteries for selfish gain, to garner admiration and respect in the eyes of men or to manipulate people into serving them in inappropriate ways that God never sanctioned. When you embrace and surrender to your assignment as a steward of God's mysteries, an undeniable, powerful and very rare **SIGNATURE** is present on your life and ministry.

A prophet also has a powerful assignment to root out, pull down and destroy all that oppose the advancement of the Gospel of Jesus Christ. This is a very strong and battle focused function of a prophet. Prophets have an assignment to contend with false prophets and demonic guards. This is why the prophet's ability to see clearly is so vitally important.

Can you imagine the damage a natural military sniper with bad eyesight would do if he was allowed to randomly shoot at things without correcting his vision? However this is the case with many prophets. They can see, but they cannot see clearly and end up taking aim at and tearing down the wrong things.

As a prophet, your ability to see clearly is directly determined by the condition of your heart. When hurts, offenses, insecurities, pride or selfish motives attack a prophet's heart, it causes what is the equivalent of dirty filters or residue over the eyes of your heart. These filters hinder clear sight and cause the prophet's passion to root out, pull down and destroy the opposition to be misguided and wrongly aimed. This wrongful aim, caused by the filters of hurts, offenses, insecurities, pride or selfish greed, leaves people damaged and hurt by prophets rather than saved and healed. Doing this literally erases the *SIGNATURE* of God from everything that prophet does and operates in.

Remembering that this facet of the assignment of the prophet is for the specific purpose of contending with false prophets and demonic guards. When a prophet allows their heart to become tainted as described above, not only do they leave a trail of hurt and damage, they also leave the demonic guard and opposition unchecked. Therefore, the prophet literally forfeits a major part of their assignment all together by not taking proper aim and focus and tearing down what they are assigned to tear down.

To better understand the prophet's assignment to root out, pull down and destroy all that oppose the advancement of the Gospel, we must look at each part of it individually. To root out means to search for and remove. When properly focused and seeing clearly, a prophet's assignment is to search for the things which are opposing the advancement of the Gospel in the areas to which they are assigned. It is like a doctor doing exploratory surgery to try to find the cause of a particular ailment for their patient, except that a prophet is searching by the Spirit in focused prayer.

The doctor takes the symptoms into consideration and according to the wisdom they have gotten in their study of medicine, they create a surgical plan to go in and find the source of the problem. As they carefully explore, when they find the source, they know exactly what to do to remove or remedy the situation. They do so carefully and with painstaking attention to detail so as to not cause damage to the surrounding tissue.

Such is the function of the prophet in the Spirit when rooting out. Like a skillful surgeon, the prophet seeks out, finds and then pulls down and destroys those things causing the ailments and oppositions to the advancement of the Gospel. This function saves lives and prospers entire regions for the Kingdom of God.

God specifically equips and gives gifts or abilities to each person according to the purpose that they are to fulfill. The role of a prophet requires great clarity and ability to see and hear accurately in order for the true purpose intended by God to be fulfilled. This is why prophets are often extremely sensitive. In fact, prophets are the most spiritually sensitive of all the five-fold ascension ministry gifts.

*"And He Himself gave some to be apostles, some prophets, some evangelists, and some pastors and teachers, for the equipping of the saints for the work of ministry, for the edifying of the body of Christ"*

**EPHESIANS 4:11-12**

The purpose of a prophet dictates the sensitivity of a prophet. With this heightened sensitivity, it is important that the prophet's ability to see remains pure and unobstructed. The condition of the prophet's heart is directly connected to the prophet's ability to see. It is vital to the prophet's purpose to keep their hearts clean and free from the limiting filters of sin, offense, frustration and selfish ambition.

Just as spiritual sensitivity is heightened for the prophet, so must be the level of consecration in their lifestyles. In order to facilitate the purity of heart required to fulfill and maximize God's purpose, a consecrated lifestyle is vital. The term "consecration" means to be set apart or dedicated to sacred purpose. It is similar to the difference between every day plates and forks and fine china and silver wear.

*"But in a great house there are not only vessels of gold and silver, but also of wood and clay, some for honor and some for dishonor. Therefore if anyone cleanses himself from the latter, he will be a vessel for honor, sanctified and useful for the Master, prepared for every good work"*

**2 TIMOTHY 2:20-21**

While normal use plates and utensils may look good, they are created for everyday use and they are not set apart in a special way. It is the exact opposite with fine china and real silverware. These items are set apart and sometimes even put on display for special occasions only. Due to their precious nature and high value, they cannot be exposed to all the same conditions as everyday plates and utensils.

They're isolated from common bumps and bruises and protected from common dust and grime. They are brought out on special occasions and handled with care because of how valuable their use is, because of how sensitive their composition is. This is a very good analogy for the LIFESTYLE of CONSECRATION that prophets must live in order to obtain and maintain a powerful signature to leave in the earth.

As a prophet you must be careful how you live and what you allow your heart to be exposed to. Like fine china, you must not be exposed to common elements. This is not to devalue or diminish those who aren't fine china and are everyday people. Everyday people are extremely precious to God in fact it is BECAUSE of them and to them that you are called as a prophet! The concept of you being like fine china compared to them as everyday plates is simply to understand that what is allowable and expedient for "everyday" people is not allowable or expedient for you as a prophet. This is because it is so extremely important for your soul to be clean and clear of as many carnal filters as possible, allowing you to hear and see clearly from the Lord.

There are three major gateways to your soul. What you SEE, what you HEAR & what you SAY are all gateways. The music you listen to, what you watch on television or movies, what you see in the news and online and even who you associate with, are all ways that your heart is being influenced and must be guarded for consecration purposes. If it isn't reflecting, resounding and repeating the Spirit of God, it is opposing the clarity of your prophetic vision and insight. This is not because you are weak, but because you are sensitive. As God's prophet, you are sensitive for great purpose and by His divine design!

At the core of living a consecrated lifestyle is a disciplined and dynamic prayer life. Your prayer life is the time you spend on a regimented and regular basis in the presence of God, seeking His face, worshipping Him and meditating in His presence and Word. Your prayer life is your life line as a prophet. It is impossible to have a prophet's signature without a powerful, active and flourishing prayer life.

As you grow in your understanding of your what it means to be a prophet, the path of your life and walk with God begins to come into a powerful focus. Many things that once seemed to be points of rejection and frustration now come into focus as places of guidance and protection because of your prophetic calling. Knowing your purpose and the requirements of it raises the standards in your life and serves as a guard against confusion.

Prophets are uncommon. Prophets who carry the signature of God must be humble and submitted to God and His authority. Prophets who are to carry God's Signature must live disciplined, diligent lifestyles... on purpose.

# CHAPTER 2
## *THE GIFTS OF THE HOLY SPIRIT*

When seeking a thorough knowledge of any topic, obtaining an understanding of **HOW** things function is equally as important as understanding **WHY** they function. In Chapter 1, we obtained a great foundational understanding of **WHY** prophets function and what the *PURPOSE* of a prophet is. In this chapter, we will begin to dissect **HOW** prophets function with a great overview of the operational *GIFTS* of the Holy Spirit.

One of the greatest joys of life is both giving and receiving gifts. In the United States alone, an estimated $280 billion dollars a year is spent in buying and giving gifts! That is in the United States alone, not including other nations. $280 billion not million, but billion! Gift giving accounts for approximately 10% of all retail spending in the United States each year.

When it comes to giving gifts to loved ones, much thought and consideration often goes into selecting the right gift for the person. Likes and dislikes, sizes, styles, preferences and interests are all painstakingly taken into consideration. In the same way that we carefully chose the right gift for the right person, God our Father chooses gifts for each of us and assigns us to the Body of Christ according to the gifts He gives us.


*"If you then, being evil, know how to give good gifts to your children, how much more will your Father who is in heaven give good things to those who ask Him!"*

**Matthew 7:11**

In the same way that you take time, care and effort to give gifts to those you love, your Heavenly Father has taken even more care and effort in giving gifts to you. If you are to understand the function of a prophet, you must understand the GIFTS of God to mankind.

He specifically selects each person's gifts, according to the purpose He sends them to earth with. In the same way that it is insulting to a human gift bearer to not utilize it or to use it wrongly, it is insulting to God as our master gift giver for us to not utilize what He has given each of us.

To use our gifts improperly or to not take time to learn how our gift function properly is equally insulting. Can you imagine purchasing someone an extremely costly computer or electronic device only to have that person refuse to learn how to use it properly? How much more does it insult God who paid the ultimate price for us to have access to our gifts when we refuse to learn how to and use them properly?

The good news is, we all have been given a powerful instruction manual and always accessible master tutor with our gifts. That instruction manual is the Word of God and our master tutor is the

Holy Spirit. In addition, like Elijah and Elisha, He appoints and assigns well seasoned and reliable senior prophets to also train us in how to function properly and maximize our gifts.

*"Whenever one does not understand the purpose of a thing, abuse is inevitable"*

Dr Myles Munroe

The first important step to value and honor properly your own gift as well as the gifts of others, is to first understand the types of gifts, their assignments and functions as well as some key principles concerning the gifts of God. There is a tremendous diversity of gifts, and they all come from the same God for His glorious purpose on earth. No one gift is better than the other, they are simply different in function but the same in origin.

The first book of Corinthians establishes for us proper understanding of the **GIFTS** of the Holy Spirit. As we seek to gain insight and understanding of these gifts, we must first ask our selves the vital question, what is a GIFT? By definition a GIFT is a thing given freely to someone without payment. A GIFT is also a natural ability or talent.

*"For to one is given the word of wisdom through the Spirit, to another the word of knowledge through the same Spirit, to another faith by the same Spirit, to another GIFTS of healings by the same Spirit, to another the working of miracles, to another prophecy, to another discerning of spirits, to another different kinds of tongues, to another the interpretation of tongues. But one and the same Spirit works all these things, distributing to each one individually as He wills"*

**1 CORINTHIANS 12:8-11**

A primary component is to understand that the GIFTS of God cannot be purchased. Your gifts were hand selected by God for your purpose. The responsibility to discover them within and operate in them is yours, but in order for a thing to be considered a gift, it cannot be purchased by the recipient.

In America, when children are small, some parents will give their children money around Christmas, Mothers or Fathers Day in order for them to allow the child to purchase a gift for them. It is normal for parents of small children to do so because the child often does not have resources of his or her own in order to buy the parent a GIFT.

While it is normal for a small child to receive money from the parent to buy the parent a GIFT, in essence, the parent is actually buying themselves something and allowing the child to pick it out. Of course the parent is still touched and receives the item as a GIFT because their small child picked it out in love for them.

However if an adult was to ask you for money to purchase a "gift" for you, how would you feel? Insulted? I would much rather buy myself something I know I will like than to give another adult my money to buy me something, unless it is that person's profession to choose things for others. Regardless, if you have to pay for it yourself, it is not a GIFT!

The proof point here is that the GIFTS of the Holy Spirit cannot be purchased by the bearer. THEY ARE REAL GIFTS! These GIFTS are freely given to those to whom they are assigned. You cannot admire another's gift and decide to go get it.

Neither can you pay enough, through an offering or the like, to receive a GIFT from the Holy Spirit. Why? Because it is a GIFT! The gifts of God are freely given and while you can miss discovering, developing or benefitting from them, you can not earn them nor can you lose them.

*"For the gifts and the calling of God are irrevocable"*

**Romans 11:29**

Another facet of understanding the gifts of God is that a GIFT is also a NATURAL TALENT or ABILITY. The gift you receive from the Holy Spirit is not determined by much you like doing something, rather it is determined by how WELL you DO something, or in other words your ability to actually do it. Many people ADMIRE the gifts that others possess. However this admiration of a gift does not make it your own.

You can WANT to possess any of the the nine gifts mentioned in 1 Corinthians, but it does not mean you actually possess it. There is no greater insult to the giver of a gift than to put it aside and ignore the one you have been given in order to admire and desire what someone else has. You cannot make yourself a prophet. You cannot make yourself a pastor, a healer, or a worker of miracles, although many try to, their best attempts produce imitation and not authentic anointing.

A great natural example of this is the difference between a real professional singer and one who wants to sing. One has a NATURAL ABILITY and talent, the other does not. One flows and makes singing look effortless, the other strains and tries their hardest, but its just not there. One moves people and touches their heart when they sing. The other repels people and hurts their ears! WANTING to sing does not make you a singer, you have to actually have the gift. Of course they can take lessons and train to perfect their gift, but they did have the core gift to begin with.

In the same way, you can want to be a prophet, pastor, etc, but you must take into consideration whether this is what God has called you to do.    It is true that you are often drawn to those who possess and are operating in the gift you also possess but the key is that it is the Holy Spirit drawing you and leading you in that way.

There is one thing you can be assured in, we are all called to be SERVANTS. You can never go wrong serving in the Kingdom of God. In fact, it is the primary way to reveal to yourself what gifts you possess and where God has called you to be.

This key of serving to reveal your gift is one that many in the body of Christ are missing. It's a worldly mentality that says, let me determine what I am good at, what I like doing and then I will see if I have time to serve. However a Kingdom mentality seeks assignment and looks for the areas of need in their church or in the ministries they are assigned to.

Kingdom mentality understands that God is in control and that needs being presented are large indicators of opportunity to tap into hidden gifts. This has nothing to do with what you like the most or prefer doing. It has to do with the heart and mindset that is willing to be a servant, to serve where needed and to allow the demand to reveal the gifts. Could it be that the reason why you don't know your true gifts and talents is because you've never allowed serving in seemingly unrelated or even small ways to reveal to you your hidden gifts and talents?

Now, as we continue to look into the gifts of the Holy Spirit, open your heart for Him to show you what your gifts are, releasing who you hope to be, to embrace who you really are. Never allow your admiration of someone's gift to cause you to TRY to imitate and operate in a gift that you have not actually been given. At best you will look ridiculous by trying to pretend you have something that you do not have while failing to discover the talents you actually do possess.

Returning now to gaining a better understanding of the God given gifts to the Body of Christ, we'll take a deeper look at the Scripture again. As listed, there are nine gifts referred to in 1 Corinthians 12, each with its own function and assignment. Each of the gifts are different and each one is equally as important. This principle of understanding the diversity of gifts is vitally important towards keeping the right heart and focus when operating in the gift or gifts that you have been given.

Again, it is important to understand that all of the nine gifts are given to us by God, as He determines, according to our assignments on earth. Your gifts, talents, anointing and authority is released from heaven in specific correlation with your God given assignment. It is specifically expressed to us in this Biblical chapter that there are "diversities of ministries" but it is the same God working through all of us.

*"For to one is given the word of wisdom through the Spirit, to another the word of knowledge through the same Spirit, to another faith by the same Spirit, to another GIFTS of healings by the same Spirit, to another the working of miracles, to another prophecy, to another discerning of spirits, to another different kinds of tongues, to another the interpretation of tongues. But one and the same Spirit works all these things, distributing to each one individually as He wills"*

**1 CORINTHIANS 12:8-11**

The most essential concept to understand in all of 1 Corinthians 12 is that while each person is unique and different in their gifting and assignment, we are all of the same Holy Spirit; all of equal importance. This understanding removes the elevation of some of the gifts over others and allows all people to embrace whichever assignment and gifting God has given them while properly appreciating the assignment and gifting of others that are different than them.

The nine gifts of the Holy Spirit that we see in 1 Corinthians 12 can be grouped into three categories for better understanding: the *POWER* gifts, the *REVELATION* gifts and the *UTTERANCE* gifts. In the following chapters we will take a more in depth look at each of these categories. We will conclude this chapter by only touching upon what the categories are.

In the most basic, simple explanation of each of these categories: The *POWER* gifts **do** something. They are a display of God's power on earth. The gifts in this category include the gift of faith, the gift of healing and the working of miracles.

The *REVELATION* gifts **know** something. They are a display of God's infinite WISDOM on earth. The gifts in this category include the gift of the Word of Wisdom, the Word of Knowledge and the Discerning of Spirits.

The *UTTERANCE* gifts **say** something. They display the VOICE of God on the earth. The gifts in this category include the gift of prophesy, the gift of tongues and the gift of the interpretation of tongues.

Whatever their function POWER, REVELATION or UTTERANCE, all are GIFTS from the Holy Spirit to mankind for Kingdom redemption. Their purpose is equal as is their importance. The gift of faith is just as important as the gift of working miracles, or prophesying, etc.

Many people do operate in more than one of these gifts and in some occasions all of them are in one person! It is rare but it does happen. The important thing to understand is that where much is given, much is required.

Whatever GIFTS you have been given, you are responsible for. You must STEWARD these gifts; developing them and using them wisely for the advancement of the Kingdom of Heaven.

*"...to another faith by the same Spirit, to another gifts of healings by the same Spirit..."*

**1 CORINTHIANS 12:9-10**

# CHAPTER 3

*THE POWER GIFTS*

There are three of the nine gifts of the Holy Spirit that are listed in 1 Corinthians 12 that are considered *POWER* gifts. These three are:

1. The gift of *FAITH*

2. The gift of *HEALING*

3. The gift of *WORKING* of *MIRACLES*.

These are the gifts that *DO* something that can be discerned by the five senses and display the power of God in a tangible way on the earth. The operation of *POWER* gifts produces belief in even the most doubting hearts and often results in a reverent awe of the realness of God's existence and presence amongst mankind. Most displays of these POWER gifts are a combination of the gifts of the Spirit working together, all for the common cause of inspiring faith in God and confidence in and reverence of His power.

The first of the power gifts we will discuss is the gift of faith. Faith is one of the most frequently used terms of the Bible. It is a concept that is widely accepted but vaguely defined in most of Christianity. This leads to many misconceptions of what faith really is.

To some, faith only refers to the belief that God exists. To others it is to believe specifically in Jesus Christ as Lord and Savior. These are both accurate displays of faith and fundamental truths, however faith has very different elements and levels of belief.

A search for the definition of faith in the Biblical text reveals that there are several Greek and Hebrew words that were translated into

42

the English word "faith." Jesus Himself referred to some people's doubt and unbelief as having "little faith." He then complimented others faith as being "great faith." In parables He spoke of faith the tiny size of a mustard seed being powerful enough to cause one's words to make mountains be uprooted and thrown into oceans!

*"Faith is the substance of things hoped for, the evidence of things not seen"*

**Hebrews 11:1**

The actual spiritual "gift of faith" that we are referring to is a supernatural faith. It is a faith that, outside of our human will, empowers us to believe what would normally be considered impossible. Every believer has a measure of faith.

When referencing "little" faith, Jesus rebuked people for doubting in the midst of challenging circumstances. On the contrary, when He referenced "great" faith, it was a compliment. He referred to how strongly and desperately they believed, despite opposition.

*"And what more shall I say? For the time would fail me to tell of Gideon and Barak and Samson and Jephthah, also of David and Samuel and the prophets: who through FAITH subdued kingdoms, worked righteousness, obtained promises, stopped the mouths of lions, quenched the violence of fire, escaped the edge of the sword, out of weakness were made strong, became valiant in battle, turned to flight the armies of the aliens. Women received their dead raised to life again. Others were tortured, not accepting deliverance, that they might obtain a better resurrection"*

**Hebrews 11:32-35**

When the gift of faith is in operation, it causes the person to see beyond what the natural eyes can see and to believe beyond what natural minds can comprehend. It causes natural limitations to fade and the reality of the sovereign power of God to become so magnified, that a force is released that causes the manifestation of their faith.

Faith moves people to take action upon the things that they are inspired to believe for. These are often the type of actions that they would normally never dream of taking. When the gift of faith is in operation, people are supernaturally empowered to believe and do great things!

The second of the power gifts is the gift of healing. It is the healing power of God demonstrated through the manifestation of various types of healing. From terminal illnesses that medicine cannot treat, to the simplest ailments of a common headache or cold, the power gift of healing is seen when physical sicknesses and ailments are supernaturally alleviated and removed. Although often manifested in physical healing, this gift is also displayed in emotional and mental healing as well.

Healing is a true priority of JESUS as it inspires faith in many people to believe in the care and supernatural intervention of God in their everyday lives. While Jesus walked on earth, His ministry was marked significantly with the flow of healing. It was through these healings that the word of His ministry spread across the region where

He walked, bringing thousands of people to His teachings and many to follow Him.

A person who is anointed with the power gift of healing is marked with manifested healing of the sick upon them operating in their times of ministry, whether they be public or private. This comes in many ways from healing flowing through the crowd while one is preaching or ministering prophetically, or through doing an altar call, anointing with oil and the laying on of hands in specific prayer.

*The centurion answered and said, "Lord, I am not worthy that You should come under my roof. But only speak a word, and my servant will be healed.*

**Matthew 8:7**

Healing can be immediate where the sick person is instantly alleviated of all symptoms and sources of their illness. There are many testimonies of cancerous tumors disappearing and chronic pain being completely alleviated. Then there are the astonishing examples where uneven limbs grow out to normal length or those physically declared dead coming back to life.

All of these are seen when the gift of healing is in operation. Deaf ears have been opened and blind eyes made to see.    Immediate healing is an extremely impactful display of the power of God!

While these immediate examples of healing are awe inspiring, it can also be a gradual change that was initiated by the touch of God's power.    This happens when God touches the sick person in a way that changes the flow of sickness in their body to a flow of health.    Those experiencing gradual healing can be totally healed within hours after the power encounter to days or even weeks.

One thing is definitive with this gradual flow of healing. The sick person's symptoms were bad and getting worse and when God touched their bodies, they immediately started getting better, moment by moment, until the healing is complete.    With gradual healing, tremendous improvement can be seen as time goes by.

Whether the healing is immediate or gradual, once a person is touched and healed by God, they are forever impacted by the display of His power. Not only does it touch the person who experienced the healing but to all who know the person, faith in God is the result.

We see this displayed in the Word of God on many occasions. Such as when Lazarus was raised from the dead in John 11. Those that witnessed this amazing display of healing went from being doubters and persecutors to passionate believers! This is exactly what the display of the power gifts is all about.

The third power gift is the gift of the working of miracles. The working of miracles is displayed when the very laws of nature are interrupted in a way that is traceable and noted. There are several Biblical historical accounts of these types of miracles, such as when time stood still for Joshua, or when Moses parted the Red Sea.

There is an account when the Prophet Elijah ran faster on foot than Ahab's chariot was going with horse power! It was physically impossible for the man of God to run faster than a horse, so fast in fact, that he was able to catch up to him and run along side him!

There is also the time when Jesus turned water into wine at a wedding feast. There is no physical way for regular water to instantly become wine. The Biblical record says that it was not just regular quality wine either. It was what the guests reflected upon and said was the best quality wine. Fine wine becomes fine because of the years that it was aged.

There is no such thing as wine without some sort of fruit, usually grapes that are given time to ferment to produce the wine and then the intentional aging process begins to produce the better wine. The laws of nature were altered in an instant in Jesus' first recorded miracle, turning the water to wine at the wedding feast at the urging of his mother.

In 2 Kings 6 there is a story of the prophet Elisha whose servant was cutting trees along the river Jordan. The servant's axe head flew off and fell into the river. He cried out to Elisha about it because he had borrowed it.

Elisha threw a stick into the water and the axe head floated to the top! There is no physical possibility that would allow an axe head made of iron to float like a piece of drift wood. This is the operation of working of miracles.

There are many more examples of the gift of working miracles both Biblical accounts and even modern testimonies. From the tremendous account of when Joshua commanded and saw the sun and moon stand still to everyday common but yet miraculous testimonies. One popular preacher who has many years of ministry experience recently shared about being a young preacher with very little money, traveling from city to city by car to preach the Gospel.

He had reached the end of his natural resources meaning he had no money. His car needed gas and he had other cities to get to in order to preach. Crying out to God, he spoke to his car and told it to not run out of gas until he had the money to fill his tank.

He drove around for hundreds of miles from city to city for an entire seven days before he finally got the money to put gas in his car! That is a contemporary example of a working miracle!

Regardless of the category, when we see the power and the spirit of God flowing, it is often a combination of the gifts of the Spirit working together. These gifts display the reality of God's ability and willingness to touch the lives of men with His power.

# CHAPTER 4
## *THE REVELATION GIFTS*


The REVELATION Gifts of the Spirit display God's infinite wisdom in the affairs of men on the earth. Revelation gifts are those that KNOW something, revealed by God to them, that they would otherwise have no knowledge of. This is the supernatural display of the ***KNOWLEDGE*** of God.

*"And now I have told you before it comes, that when it does come to pass, you may believe"*

**JOHN 14:29**

Three of the nine gifts of the Holy Spirit that are listed in 1 Corinthians 12 are considered **REVELATION** gifts. These three are:

1. The gift of **WORD OF WISDOM**

2. The gift of **WORD OF KNOWLEDGE**

3. The gift of **DISCERNING OF SPIRITS**

The first of the REVELATION gifts we will discuss is the Word of Wisdom. The Spiritual Gift of the Word of Wisdom is the operation of the gifts in the form of prophesies that speak of the future. It speaks to something that is coming or is about to happen. This is normally something that would not be personally known to the one operating in the gift.

Wisdom reveals what is to happen and often how to handle it. God releases these types of words to prepare you for what is coming. He also causes this revelatory gift to flow to inspire people to believe and know that He is involved and cares about their every day lives.

One of the greatest examples of this was when Joseph interpreted Pharoah's dream according to the Biblical historical account. Joseph's story in the book of Genesis is very rich with many Kingdom principles. His story is one of the greatest examples concerning the process that must be endured to walk in the purpose and vision that God has for your life.

However for this chapter we will focus on when Joseph operated in the Word of Wisdom upon interpreting Pharaoh's dream. The Pharaoh was the king of Egypt. At that time, Egypt was the superpower nation of their day. Pharaoh was troubled by a dream that he had, that none of his experts or spiritual advisors could get the proper interpretation for.

In his distress to know the dream, one of his aides recommended a master dream interpreter by the name of Joseph who had been forgotten in the prison. Joseph was brought to Pharaoh, and not only did he flow in dream interpretation and tell Pharaoh the meaning of his vexing dream, but Joseph operated heavily in the Word of Wisdom revealing the plan for how to handle the warning given by God in the dream.

By functioning in the Word of Wisdom, Joseph gave a financial plan for how to handle the current years of plenty that would be followed by a severe season of drought and poverty. Operating in the Word of Wisdom, God revealed a plan through Joseph that involved setting a specific percentage aside during the years of plenty that would carry them through the years of impending drought.

There is no way Joseph could have come up with this information on his own accord instantly. Joseph had the Word of Wisdom flowing through him. By heeding the Word of Wisdom, they ended up saving their nation when others crumbled and thousands in other nations were dying of starvation and dehydration.

One who flows in the Word of Wisdom is a great asset to any company, family, church or government that they serve. The wisdom they flow in is not the wisdom of men or their own wisdom. It is the wisdom of God, the creator and source of all things. His wise solutions and plans are fail proof and can save companies, families, churches or even entire nations.

The second of the REVELATION gifts is the Word of Knowledge. The Word of Knowledge, although closely related to the Word of Wisdom, is specifically different. When a Word of Knowledge comes forth, it is a prophesy that speaks of the past and the present.

The Word of Wisdom speaks to the future, the Word of Knowledge speaks to the past and present. This knowledge is information that would not be naturally known to the person who is operating in the gifts of the Holy Spirit. It is supernaturally given by God to the one sharing it.

When you are flowing in the Word of Knowledge you know something about the person and what they are going through or what they have been through that you would have otherwise not have known or been told about them. The function and flow of this gift can bring tremendous healing and release when in proper operation.

A person who flows in the gift of knowledge will often get a Word for people as they are passing them in the store or on the street.

While riding a train or working on your job, God will reveal to you what is happening in someone's life and possibly what they are dealing with or dabbling in.

Sometimes the Word of Knowledge reveals the person's situation for you to pray for them. Other times it is for you to help them in a specific way. And on occasion, it maybe for you to confront or correct them.

Every Word of Knowledge is not always meant to be shared. There are times it is for you to intercede and pray for the situation. Other times you will feel compelled by the Spirit of God to share with the person what He has shown you.

Even when the Lord prompts you to share it, it is not always meant to be in its entirety. You may sometimes share only a portion of what God has shown you. Whether you share nothing, a portion or an entirety, God's REASON, His PURPOSE in giving you the Word of Wisdom is either to impact the person or to warn you about them and sometimes it is both!

When it is for the purpose of impacting the person, the Word of Knowledge brings awe and often relief. Awe in the fact that God is so particularly aware of their situation, that He knows where they are and what they've been through.

Relief in the fact that He loves them so much that He would speak to their situation. The Word of Knowledge and the flow of healing and deliverance often come together. The Word of Knowledge paves the way in the person's soul for healing and deliverance to flow.

There are also times when the Word of Knowledge reveals to you what a person is involved with as a way to warn you about them. The warning could be for you to simply avoid allowing the person access to your life in ways that could prove to be damaging. In cases where you see that a person is dabbling or functioning in the occult or where there are other demonic spirits at work in them, it could also be to have you stand against whatever they are trying to do by interceding and taking authority in the Spirit. This goes hand in the hand with the final of the revelatory gifts, the gift of the discerning of spirits.

The final REVELATION gift is the Gift of Discerning of Spirits. To discern by definition means to detect with senses other than natural vision or to know or recognize mentally. Therefore to operate by the

Holy Spirit in the Gift of Discernment means that God is supernaturally revealing what spirit is in operation.

In any given situation with a person, there are three potential spirits at work. It can be the Holy Spirit, a demon spirit(s) or the human spirit. The Gift of Discernment reveals which one is in operation. All three have a voice!

The human spirit refers to the person who is being led by their own selfish or carnal desires. When this spirit is leading the entire purpose is to gratify one's own will and desires. It flows strongly in conjunction with the person's ego. They can try to mask it with kind words or stated good intentions, but the spirit of discernment causes you to see past the surface to recognize self serving intent.

A demon spirit has the purpose of the devil as his intention and seeks to bring division, confusion, sin and oppression. There is a heaviness that is tangible when this kind of spirit is in operation. Some who are particularly sensitive prophetically can even feel physically ill when a heavy demonic presence is being discerned.

The enemy hates the advancement of the truth of the Gospel. Someone functioning in this spirit is always trying to hinder truth from being revealed and advancing, ultimately to cause disharmony and deception to flow.

Finally while the other two may try to imitate His presence and leading, there is the powerful and pure flow of the Holy Spirit of God. When the Holy Spirit is flowing there is a marked peace and often a tangible stirring or quickening that is felt. There is nothing better than being in the presence of the Holy Spirit and among those who are flowing in Him.

The gift of DISCERNMENT of spirits is a extremely vital one. Especially for those who are called in ministry of any kind. The realm you operate in is the spirit realm. To try to operate in ministry, which is in essence to do work in the spirit realm and not have the gift of discernment is like trying to be a truck driver with no eyesight. It would not take long before a terrible wreck would be the result!

*"And He spoke a parable to them: "Can the blind lead the blind? Will they not both fall into the ditch?"*

**Luke 6:39**

Flowing in the gift of discernment allows you to see and know both who and what you are dealing with. It allows you to see beyond the surface and not go simply by impressions, which can be mistaken and wrong. Discernment and judgement are two closely related but very different things.

The Bible warns us to avoid passing judgment on people, stressing that to whatever degree we judge others is the degree to which we subject ourselves to be measured and judged. The same Bible also admonishes us to "know those who labor amongst us."

Discernment involves recognizing the source of the influence a person is under. Discerning a situation or person properly opens the doors to the wisdom and plan of God to prevail in any given circumstance. When it is absent the opposite is also true, the enemy is given open access to bring destruction.

The flowing of the Revelatory gifts of God are incredibly vital to mankind in an incredibly powerful way. Humans are designed by the mind of God and created by the thoughts of God. The fact that you were born, everything about you, is the proof of a series of thoughts that was on God's MIND! There is a law in physics that says anything that is created within an environment must stay within that environment to both thrive and survive.

Therefore, if you were created in the MIND and PRESENCE of God, that means you are designed not just to survive but to also thrive by REMAINING in His mind and His presence. This is exactly why these REVELATORY GIFTS are of such vast importance.

There are millions of people both believers and non believers that are struggling in life because they aren't living in the environment for which they were designed live and thrive in, which is the mind of God. The world desperately needs to hear, see and know the mind of God.

This is why the Revelatory Gifts are so important! Whether it be the word of knowledge, wisdom or the discerning of Spirits, when we flow in the Revelatory gifts of God, we usher ourselves and those who hear us into the environment we need to survive and thrive. It is why when people experience these revelatory gifts and the presence of God that come with them, even those who are not particularly emotional people will have a very emotional response.

They are experiencing their original environment of creation for the first time!  In the natural this compares to the often very moving experience of being born and raised in a country other than that of your own national origin and then visiting your nation as an adult for the first time.  Many African Americans have testimonies of the deeply emotional experience of visiting Africa for the first time and being very surprised by how deeply emotional it was for them.

When the revelatory gifts of God are flowing, you are serving as an ambassador or tour guide for people to experience their birth nation for the first time.  You release to people, often indirectly, a sense of identity and belonging.

# CHAPTER 5
## *THE UTTERANCE GIFTS*

The final of the gifting categories is called the UTTERANCE GIFTS. The Utterance Gifts are those that SAY something. When these gifts are in operation, what is known to the mind and spirit by the revelation gifts are openly made known unto those who hear. As with all the manifestation of the gifts of God, when in operation, faith in and reverence of God are the tangible results.

As with the other categories of the gifts of the Holy Spirit, the Utterance Gifts have three within this category. Each of these gifts are so closely related that they can be difficult to understand the difference between. In addition, they almost always operate together.

While closely related and defined, in gaining a proper understanding of prophets and prophesy, it is important to understand the subtle differences between each one. The three gifts in this category are:

1. Gift of Prophesy

2. Gift of Tongues

3. Gift of Interpretation of Tongues

The first and most important of the three utterance gifts is the simple gift of prophesy. It is most important of all three of the gifts in this category. The gift of prophesy exists and flows for the singular purpose of edifying the local church.

The pure, simple gift of prophesy is what is called "forth-telling" and has no "foretelling" revelation in it. The misunderstanding of the difference in those two functions has caused the flow of the gift of prophesy in the modern church to have been both misunderstood and manipulated greatly.

At best, this results in well intentioned but often misguided demonstrations of this gift. At worst, it results in a demonic flow of divination and witchcraft where people are manipulated and lead astray. The latter has them seeking what is the equivalent of psychic, demonic insight rather than the pure edification of forth-telling the will, heart and mind of God. This is the real God intended purpose of the gift of prophesy.

FORTH-TELLING means to "utter forth." It means to declare something that can only be known by divine revelation. Forth-telling serves to reveal God's will and to interpret His purposes to those who hear it. In it's pure form, prophesy's purpose is to make known the truth of God to men.

FORETELLING is very different. It involves declaring specific future events that have not been yet revealed. The pure, simple gift of prophecy is always forth-telling and has no foretelling revelation in it.

It speaks to men for edification, exhortation and comfort. If prophecy does not build up, strengthen or comfort, it is not prophecy.

> *"Pursue love, and desire spiritual gifts, but especially that you may prophesy. For he who speaks in a tongue does not speak to men but to God, for no one understands him; however, in the spirit he speaks mysteries. But he who prophesies speaks edification and exhortation and comfort to men"*
>
> **1 Corinthians 14:1-3**

The second gift in the category of utterance gifts is the gift of tongues. It is important to understand that the actual gift of tongues is not to be confused with a human's spirit talking to God in prayer in an inarticulate language. That is often referred to as our prayer language or our heavenly language. All believers who are baptized in the Holy Spirit can speak in other tongues to edify themselves in prayer.

It is understood that when we are praying in our heavenly prayer language, the Holy Spirit is interceding for us and through us. The

Bible refers to us not always knowing exactly what we need to pray for in our life situations at any given time. However the Holy Spirit does know exactly what we need.

When we are praying in our heavenly language, the Holy Spirit is bypassing our conscious, aware minds and interceding for us through utterance that we ourselves do not understand. The purpose is for our personal edification and individual spiritual benefit. This is different than the gift of tongues which operates in a local assembly.

The gift of tongues is demonstrated in the local church assembly when God wants to edify that local congregation and not necessarily a specific person or targeted individual. It is an utterance in an unknown tongue or language, one that is foreign to those who are present. During a break or an appropriate time during a local church service, a person is heard with a specifically different sounding unknown language.

The sound is often authoritarian. It stands out in the general assembly and a reverent hush will fall on those who hear it. In contrast, a heavenly language is for personal prayer only, the audience and interaction occurring between the person and God directly.

The gift of tongues is for the public church assembly and has nothing to do with the direct benefit of the one operating in it. For this gift to be in proper Biblical order as a prophetic utterance it must be accompanied by the next gift in this category, the gift of the interpretation of tongues.

The gift of the interpretation of tongues is when another believer standing by openly interprets the unknown tongue. It can also be the same person who brought forth the unknown tongue who interprets it immediately after bringing it forth. To "interpret" means to speak in the known language of the local assembly and share precisely what the unknown tongue meant. When the unknown tongue and the interpretation of it flow together, it becomes the gift of prophecy for the local assembly. Tongues alone is not prophesy unless it is coupled with proper interpretation.

The gift of prophecy can happen when the gift of tongues and interpretation flow together or it can occur of its own accord as the Holy Spirit leads. The gift of prophesy is a supernatural utterance in a known tongue. To prophesy means to "flow forth" or to "bubble forth" like a fountain and "to speak."

One who prophesies will deliver the mind, will and purpose of God in our lives. The simple gift of prophecy always edifies those who hear the message. To edify means to "instruct and improve in moral and spiritual knowledge"

We must be careful not to confuse the simple gift of prophesy with the ascension, five-fold ministry gift of being an actual prophet. This is also often referred to as the office of the prophet. The fact that someone prophesies does not make him or her a official five-fold ascension prophet. According to Scripture, anyone can prophesy.

*For you can all prophesy one by one, that all may learn and all may be encouraged.*

**1 Corinthians 14:31**

This is displayed in many examples in Biblical history. There are several accounts of the Spirit of God coming upon common men or women and them prophesying powerfully. This did not mean they were prophets, holding the office of prophet of God.

The actual office of the prophet of God is a specific, hand picked assignment from God. This is the person's identity, purpose and calling rather than the flowing of a spiritual gift alone. Great examples of this are when God called the prophet Samuel or the prophet Jeremiah. They are both actual prophets, their identities were revealed to them when they received their calling.

In contrasting comparison, David was called as a king of Israel. However there are accounts of when the Spirit of God came upon David and he prophesied alongside the prophets of his day. David was called as a king. God described David as a man after His own heart. However him flowing in the gift of prophesy did not make David an actual prophet.

Those who hold the actual calling and office of a prophet flow in all of utterance gifts in order to be a fully mantled prophet. When a true Prophet prophesies, they will also have two, if not all three of the Revelation Gifts in operation in their lives also.

It is not a one time or special occurrence to the prophet. The gifts of revelation and utterance all flowing together is normal for the five-fold prophet. Again the three revelation gifts are the word of knowledge, the word of wisdom and the discerning of spirits. Those ordained by God as prophets flow readily in the revelation gifts, the utterance gifts and can function both in forth-telling and foretelling prophesy.

As we seek to understand God's assignment in our lives, and pursue His mind on how to leave a prophetic signature in the earth, we must each embrace who we are created to be. Just as your natural signature is unique to you as a person, so is your assignment given to you by God.

The utterance gifts of God are so extremely precious to the function of faith in the earth, that God causes both those who are prophets and those who are not to flow in these gifts according to His will and purpose.

# CHAPTER 6
## *THE SIGNATURE OF PRAYER*

To the prophet, a prayer life is not optional. It is of the utmost importance and is essentially vital the life and ministry of the prophet. Prayer is your direct communication and link with God.

As a prophet you are His spokesperson. You stand as His representation in the earth. Therefore, when you speak, you are speaking on His behalf. You work for Him and Him alone. Your directives, initiatives and orders come from God directly.

In order to fulfill your assignment duties as a prophet, you must strive to always be in tune with Him at all times. This is only achieved through the avenue and discipline of prayer. Prayer is the only avenue by which mankind can stay in tune and in focus with God's heart and mind.

A prophet without a prayer life is like a corporate executive that refuses to show up at the office or read any reports concerning how the company is performing. How could that executive do their job properly if they never show up to work? How can they make decisions on the proper direction or planning for the company if they refuse to see or know anything that is happening at the company?

Prayer is how you stay connected and in tune with God at all times, your line of communication with Him. It is how you know what is happening and how to handle what is happening. Prayer is spending time with God and communicating with Him. It is meditating on His Word and in His presence.

By having a committed and consistent prayer life, you get to know Him more intimately. You begin to fine tune your spiritual ears to the specific sound of His voice. His ways and thoughts become familiar to you and you know His presence because you are accustomed to it.

*"The effective, fervent prayer of a righteous man avails much. Elijah was a man with a nature like ours, and he prayed earnestly that it would not rain; and it did not rain on the land for three years and six months. And he prayed again, and the heaven gave rain, and the earth produced its fruit"*

**James 5:16-18**

Prayer is not just a discipline, it is also a skill. HOW we pray is just as important as WHAT we pray or how often we do it. The Biblical historical account of the prophet Elijah is a classic example of a man who knew HOW to pray. It serves as our lesson for the mechanics and skill of prayer. In fact, many centuries before prayer was written about in the book of James, we find its fulfillment in the prophet Elijah.

This mention in the book of James of the prophet Elijah's prayer life refers to the historical account given in 1 Kings 18:41-46. As God's mouthpiece and representative, Elijah new the voice and character of God so well that he could hear and see what no one else could. This was a testament to the strength of Elijah's prayer life.

As we dissect Elijah's prayer in this wonderful account, there are some insightful principles on prophetic prayer that we can glean from. The first principle is that Elijah prayed in FAITH.

*"Then Elijah said to Ahab, "Go up, eat and drink; for there is the sound of abundance of rain."*

**1 Kings 18:41**

What exactly was it that Elijah heard? No one else seemed to hear a sound of rain in the natural, nor did they see it. The truth is that while there was no natural indication that any rain was going to fall in any part of Israel. Elijah was hearing, seeing and knowing by FAITH.

As a prophet, when you pray, you must pray in **unwavering faith**. If we are praying for something to happen, we need to KNOW, with assurance, that it WILL happen. Simply put, to pray effectively, we must believe!

> *"So Jesus answered and said to them, "Have faith in God. For assuredly, I say to you, whoever says to this mountain, 'Be removed and be cast into the sea,' and does not doubt in his heart, but believes that those things he says will be done, he will have whatever he says. Therefore I say to you, whatever things you ask when you pray, believe that you receive them, and you will have them"*

**Mark 11:22-24**

Having faith and believing in the promises of the Word of God is the primary principle of prayer. Notice in verse 24, the instructions are in past tense. We are to believe that we have already received what it is we are praying for. It is at the point of BELIEF that it becomes ours.

Elijah operated in total faith. He heard the rain by faith. Immediately he began to operate from that place of total faith before he saw the actual manifestation of it on the earth. The backbone of your prayer life is your faith! This is why it is so vital that you believe, that you starve your doubts and feed your faith by spending time with God and in His Word. As His mouthpiece, people's lives and well being are dependent upon your prayer life!

The second prayer principle we can gather from the prophet Elijah's example is that he prayed in *HUMILITY*. In 1 Kings 18:42 it is displayed for us Elijah's stance of proper prophetic prayer. It says that he told Ahab to go, eat and drink while he went to the top of Mount Carmel. There, he bowed down on his face before God, placing his face to the ground between his knees.

As a prophet of God, when you are going into prayer to produce the will and mind of God in earthy manifestation, submission to the process and humility in your approach are vital components. Notice that Ahab was given the instructions to go ahead and begin to now eat and drink like it had already happened, but the prophet of God then denied himself and pressed into prayer.

You must be willing to be humble and selfless enough to recognize that you will often deliver a Word to someone to go ahead and celebrate the breakthrough, while you yourself are yet laboring for it in prayer. This requires a level of humility and focus that many refuse to operate in. It is also why there are so few prophetic signatures in the earth in our generation.

The next principle of prophetic prayer we can glean from Elijah is the principle of persistence in prayer. Persistence is defined as "continuing firmly or obstinately in a course of action in spite of difficulty or opposition." Elijah had asked his servant to go and see if there was any evidence of manifestation of rain yet. The report came back more than once that there was no evidence of manifestation.

Despite the difficulty or opposition, Elijah persisted in prayer. He sent the servant to look for evidence of manifestation time and time again. He persisted until the report came back of a tiny cloud the size of a man's hand.

Elijah prayed definitely and specifically. He focused on what he knew was the will and mind of God for that season. He pressed into it, not deviating from what he knew was the promise for that season for Israel.

In this same way, as a prophet you must be willing to bow down and commit to the process of persisting in prayer for the things which you are assigned to give birth to in the Spirit. When the natural circumstances do not immediately or initially change, the natural or habitual response is to move past whatever it is, to avoid disappointment. We are naturally wired to subconsciously avoid or move away from disappointment and hurt. As a prophet, that natural desire to let it go and move on is our enemy. We must be willing to NOT let it go and simply move on. Breakthrough often comes by persistence and perseverance in prayer!

Finally, Elijah prayed *SUCCESSFULLY*. We know that the historical account says in verses 44 and 45 that the clouds suddenly grew dark and the abundance of rain that Elijah had been praying and believing for, surely came to pass. Having the ability to pray successfully is extremely vital to your assignment as a prophet.

When our lives and efforts produce a tangible, positive result, it is referred to as being *FRUITFUL*. In the natural, we want to believe that fruitfulness is not a focus or requirement of God. It would seem that because God loves us, He would not have requirements of us to produce. However is that train of thoughts and feelings really Biblically accurate in how God's character is reflected?

There is a parable in the book of Matthew where JESUS encountered a fig tree that was bearing no fruit. He expected for the tree, even though the Bible accounts that it was not the season for it to have fruit, to be fruitful. Not only did JESUS expect the tree to be fruitful, but He expected for it to be fruitful in a non-harvest season!

The story goes on to say in some gospel records that JESUS gave the opportunity for the tree to have one last chance to become productive. He allowed those we tended the tree to fertilize it and dig around it to give it the final opportunity to be fruitful. He even left it a short space and time before He would return to see if it had PRODUCED. When JESUS returned to find it still UNFRUITFUL, He cursed the tree and commanded it to cease to exist. It immediately and instantly dried up and withered away.

It is clear that our FRUITFULNESS is very important to God. There is another story of the talents, where JESUS gave each of three servants varying amounts of talents. He expected that each servant would produce with the talents He gave them.

He didn't expect equal production, but equal effort and equal success of those efforts. One of the three didn't produce fruit. JESUS called that servant wicked and slothful.

As prophets, our prayer lives cannot be wicked and slothful; also known as unfruitful. We cannot waiver in prayer. We cannot grow weary and give up in prayer. Why? Because when God called you and sent you to earth as His prophet, He had a harvest of FRUIT on His mind. Your fruit is produced in persevering, productive prayer!

Prayer is a skill. A skill can be learned, developed and even fine tuned. However as with any skill, beyond gifting in that area, one must spend time practicing in order to become successful in our efforts. Regimens of activity produce skill and proficiency. Practice does make perfect. The more you pray, the better you become at prayer.

The capstone of this chapter on prayer is the understanding that in order for the signature of prayer to be authenticated, it must have proper guidance and motives. As a prophet you praying through to manifestation is never supposed to be about validating your ability as a prophet to get a prayer through. Prophetic prayer that produces is for the purpose of God receiving glory and sinners to take notice of Him, not us.

The motives are clear: it's not about self promotion, not to impress people, but for the sole purpose to glorify God. The manifestation of the promise was the clear goal of Elijah's prayer. He didn't invent the need, present it to God and then hoped that God would make it rain.

Elijah knew God would bring the rain as soon as he asked because he knew God's mind and what God's word said on the subject. That came from spending time with God, knowing His voice and His heart. Elijah penned his signature as a prophet and you can do the same when you pray.

# CHAPTER 7
## *THE SIGNATURE OF ANOINTING*

When you think of the word "anointing," what comes to mind? Do you think of miracles manifesting? What exactly is the Signature of Anointing? People often confuse the presence or operation of one's gifting with the presence of God's anointing. While the two SHOULD always work together, that is not always the case.

A person can be operating in their heavenly gift, which is endowed to them by God according to the purpose He has for their lives, and not necessarily be operating under the anointing. The

Biblical understanding of the anointing of God is as vital to the Christian believer as knowing one's purpose. Too often, people hear the word "anointing" and think its a feeling or display of emotion.

While the presence or encounter with the authentic anointing of God can produce feelings or displays of emotion, it is not the feeling or emotion that makes it authentic. In order to understand what authentic anointing is, you must first understand that anointing has a very specific and well defined purpose.

> *"The Spirit of the Lord is upon Me, Because He has anointed Me To preach the gospel to the poor; He has sent Me to heal the brokenhearted, To proclaim liberty to the captives and recovery of sight to the blind, To set at liberty those who are oppressed; To proclaim the acceptable year of the Lord."*
>
> **Luke 4:18-20**

The anointing of the prophet has the primary purpose of proclaiming the Gospel of Jesus Christ. It exists to break the chains of spiritual and natural poverty, to heal the broken hearted, to set the captives free and to allow the spiritually and naturally blind to see. Authentic anointing has a specific assignment and with that assignment comes spiritual authority. What distinguishes authentic ANOINTING from impressive signs and wonders gifting is SPIRITUAL AUTHORITY.

The demonstration of power gifts can be imitated however real spiritual authority cannot be imitated nor manipulated. When the demonstration of gifting is skilled, it can produce intense emotions and experiences for people. Unfortunately without spiritual AUTHORITY, lasting freedom and life impact cannot be experienced.

To understand the importance of authentic anointing which we now understand is spiritual authority, the set structure and origin of the universe must be at least generally understood. Everything that exists in the natural realm is directly connected to the spiritual realm. According to Biblical principle and historical account, everything that exists in the natural first originated in the spirit. In order for the natural to be impacted in a authentic supernatural way, the anointing/ spiritual authority is required.

*Now faith is the SUBSTANCE of things hoped for, the EVIDENCE of things not seen. For by it the elders obtained a good testimony. By faith we understand that the worlds were framed by the word of God, so that the THINGS WHICH ARE SEEN WERE NOT MADE OF THINGS WHICH ARE VISIBLE..*

**Hebrews 11:1-3**

Authentic anointing is the EVIDENCE of heavenly authority. Heavenly authority is a requirement in order to see lasting positive impact in natural life. Therefore, one of the most important things a prophet has is his or her anointing.

Remembering again that one can be GIFTED but NOT ANOINTED, it is a master key of prophets to seek God for the anointing and to understand both what causes the anointing to be strong and what causes it to falter. Otherwise your ministry will end up being entertaining but lacking real life changing anointing.

There are several principles that are important to understand about spiritual authority and anointing. The first is to understand that anointing is given as a result of assignment and as a confirmation of right positioning in the office of that assignment. Einstein once said that if you judge a fish by its ability to climb a tree it will spend its entire life believing that it is stupid.

Too many believers spend their entire lives thinking they are void of power and anointing but the reality is, they simply have not found their assignments and proper offices to occupy. In the same way one should not judge a fish by its ability to climb a tree, a believer should not judge their own abilities outside of their God given assignment and design.

Spiritual authority that releases the anointing is delegated authority. By definition, to "delegate" means to send or authorize someone to do something as a representative. Your authority is delegated by God. It is the proof of His authorization for you to function as His representative to do something. That "something" is your assignment. A person who ignores their purpose forfeits their authority. Finding your assignment comes through surrendering to the

Holy Spirit and being willing to take seriously the tasks, assignments and needs that are presented to you in your service to God's Kingdom and His house, which leads to the second principle of spiritual authority.

Specifically in the assignment of the prophet, the second principle of spiritual authority and anointing is the process of development. To develop means to grow or cause to grow and become more mature, advanced or elaborate.

For the prophet there is a process of five pillars that develop, grow and mature your anointing. These five pillars build upon one another but can also overlap one another as you walk them out and allow them to develop your anointing. The first of these pillars is mentorship.

Mentorship, in general terms, is a relationship in which a more experienced person or more knowledgeable person helps to guide a less experienced or less knowledgable person. This is especially important for someone new to their assignment and purpose as a prophet. There is an old saying, "more is caught then taught." This is best displayed in the Bible example of the prophets Elijah and Elisha.

Elijah was God's prophet. Elisha was also God's prophet. Elisha did twice the works of Elijah. His authority, his anointing was significantly larger than Elijah's. How did this happen? Was there a principle or something that Elisha did to have a greater anointing?

Young Elisha found a MENTOR in Elijah. Elijah wasn't just any mentor to Elisha. He was the God appointed mentor. For every prophetic assignment there are God appointed mentors. Mentors are have the experience, knowledge and authority/anointing to pass on to someone else.

Prophetic mentorship is not just having conversations with your mentor. Although mentors do directly share wisdom and principles, the most powerful way to receive from a prophetic mentor is to serve and sow into that mentor. Kingdom Mentorship involves serving, sowing and submitting to the mentor's example and ministry.

It requires commitment and loyalty. Elisha SERVED Elijah, even in adverse circumstances. Even when Elijah went through times of discouragement and tried to release Elisha, Elisha proved his commitment and loyalty by refusing to take the opportunity to leave.

ELISHA STAYED. He was determined to not leave Elijah. As a result, he demonstrated for all prophets the principle of the double portion anointing.

> *When they came to the other side, Elijah said to Elisha, "Tell me what I can do for you before I am taken away." And Elisha replied, "Please let me inherit a double share of your spirit and become your successor." "You have asked a difficult thing," Elijah replied. "If you see me when I am taken from you, then you will get your request. But if not, then you won't." Elisha picked up Elijah's cloak, which had fallen when he was taken up. Then Elisha returned to the bank of the Jordan River. When the group of prophets from Jericho saw from a distance what happened, they exclaimed, "Elijah's spirit rests upon Elisha!"*

> **2 Kings 2:9-10, 13, 15**

As a prophet it is imperative to seek God's face on who your God appointed mentor is. Once that is revealed, it is important in order to produce what Heaven intends, that you connect in an above average way. It is important that you connect and get involved; that you begin to serve, sow and submit.

Once you are properly connected, make a decision to commit to the entire process and to be loyal. Prophets are humans, they have personalities and quirks just like any other person. However as with any of the five fold ascension gifts, Prophets are also those who are positioned by God as His very own mouthpiece.

Each assignment carries its own anointing and authority. In order to have authority, one must be under authority. Therefore, it is very important to understand the principle of submission and service unto God, by serving and sowing into His servant. The double portion of anointing and authority is released because of your faithfulness and willingness to be under authority.

The second pillar of prophetic development is through direct teaching and training in the operation of the prophetic. This is why books like this one are so vital and important to those who are young in the prophetic. Attending in person prophetic training, such as the Signature of a Prophet Conference is invaluable.

Elijah had a school of prophets. This school was compromised of individuals who were learning from the lessons, lifestyle and ministry administration of Elijah. This takes the learning from simply reading about how to operate prophetically to getting hands on training and experience to correspond with the lessons.

In order for a person to obtain a pilot's license they must have a specific amount of textbook training or classroom experience. However no matter how well a student pilot does in the classroom, he cannot even begin to take the test for his or her license until they have hundreds of hours of flight time. This flight time is time where the student is flying next to the instructor and it cannot be skipped or excused.

In order for a pilot's license to be issued, the hundreds of hours of hands on flight training must be done. While only God controls the "licensing" of His prophets, it helps the new prophet to obtain qualified and sanctified teaching and training on how to operate in the prophetic.

The third pillar of prophetic development is through developing and establishing a profound prayer life and consecrated lifestyle.

Although this topic was thoroughly covered in the preceding chapter, it is important to understand that the Signature of a Prayer life is a vital pillar in one's development as a prophet. A consecrated lifestyle is a life that is set aside from normal lifestyle in order to be a pure vessel for God's holy purpose.

What maybe permissible for those who are not prophets, is not expedient for those who are prophets. Prophets do not have the privilege of living lives unto themselves at any time because what they do in private directly effects the signature of their anointing in public. There is nothing more saddening than seeing someone with a huge prophetic call and great gifting, sacrifice their real signature, the fullness of their anointing and authority, due to a lack of willingness and discipline in how they live their lives and establish their prayer life.

The fourth pillar of prophetic development is sanctification of the heart. Sanctification is a purging and washing out of all impurities. In all people, the condition of a person's heart will always directly effect the condition of their lives.

*Guard your heart above all else, for it determines the course of your life.*

**Proverbs 4:23**

For the prophet, this is even more detrimental. The condition of a prophet's heart doesn't just effect their own lives. The condition of a prophet's heart effects many people's lives, potentially hundreds to thousands and even millions in some cases. The greater a prophet is willing to die to self in order to sanctify their hearts for God's use, the more God can trust that prophet with greater levels of anointing and authority.

There are many things that are "natural" responses to life and circumstances that can effect the sanctification of a prophet's heart. True holy sanctification requires great internal sacrifice for the prophet. In the book of Galatians, a list of fruits of the flesh are listed in contrast to a list of fruits of the Holy Spirit. For one's heart to be truly sanctified, it must be continually purged of all fruits of the flesh.

*"Now the works of the flesh are evident, which are: adultery, fornication, uncleanness, lewdness, idolatry, sorcery, hatred, contentions, jealousies, outbursts of wrath, selfish ambitions, dissensions, heresies, envy, murders, drunkenness, revelries, and the like; of which I tell you beforehand, just as I also told you in time past, that those who practice such things will not inherit the kingdom of God.*

*But the fruit of the Spirit is love, joy, peace, longsuffering, kindness, goodness, faithfulness, gentleness, self-control. Against such there is no law. And those who are Christ's have crucified the flesh with its passions and desires. If we live in the Spirit, let us also walk in the Spirit."*

**Galatians 5:19-25**

The Word of God encourages us to judge our own fruit, to measure the condition of our souls by the fruit our lives are manifesting. These verses in Galatians are a great way to consider one's own ways and be honest with ourselves concerning whether we are operating by the Holy Spirit or by the flesh. The Spirit has a certain character that is accurately described in verse 22.

The flesh also has specific character traits, described in verses 19-21. In any given situation you can know which spirit is in operation by simply considering the fruit being displayed. Is it the Holy Spirit or is it the flesh?

Bringing back to mind the principle that the condition of your heart determines the flow coming from it, it is clear that a prophet's true consecration impacts not only his own life, but the lives of potentially millions of others. This pillar of sanctification is one that cannot be sacrificed. As you "set yourself apart" from normal life in order to be used by God, you become a vessel that God can trust and allow His anointing to flow through.

# CHAPTER 8
## *THE PROPHET & THE LOCAL CHURCH*

The fifth and final pillar of prophetic development is one that is often one of the most difficult principles to grasp in our modern society. This is the pillar of submission to authority. In a time and season in our world where illegitimate authority has become an epidemic, it is increasingly difficult to understand how and why submission to authority is not only needed but required.

However as with all the principles of God, the status quo of the society or state of the world do not change God's intentions nor requirements. Submission to authority is a universal principle of leadership that there is no way to circumvent in the Kingdom of God. God established a simple but powerful principle in order to qualify and protect the authority power/anointing that He entrusts to men.

*"Remember those who rule over you, who have spoken the word of God to you, whose faith follow, considering the outcome of their conduct. Jesus Christ is the same yesterday, today, and forever."*

**Hebrews 13:7-8**

God established His church as His set place of interaction with mankind on earth. The local church is the place where people come to connect in a corporate way with the Holy Spirit, receive lessons from the Word of God and enjoy the company and community of other like minded believers. While this is the obvious function of the local church, there is an even more profound function that many who only visit or attend church casually often miss. The local church is also the place where God's set authority is established, and His Kingdom government convenes on the earth.

*And He Himself gave some to be apostles, some prophets, some evangelists, and some pastors and teachers, for the equipping of the saints for the work of ministry, for the edifying of the body of Christ, till we all come to the unity of the faith and of the knowledge of the Son of God, to a perfect man, to the measure of the stature of the fullness of Christ;*

**Ephesians 4:11-12**

This text lays a foundation for how Kingdom authority is distributed on earth. Often referred to as the "five-fold ministry gifts" these are all offices and positions that God provided for His authority to be established on earth. It is vital to the rising prophet to understand their own position's placement in this Kingdom authority structure as well as how important being submitted to it is for their anointing and assignment to be safely established.

*Now we ask you, brothers and sisters, to appreciate those who diligently work among you [recognize, acknowledge, and respect your leaders], who are in charge over you in the Lord and who give you instruction, and [we ask that you appreciate them and] hold them in the highest esteem in love because of their work [on your behalf]. Live in peace with one another.*

**1 Thessalonians 5:12-13 AMP**

In order for a prophet to have authority, they must be under authority. You cannot possess the benefits of a system you are not submitted to. In the local church, God has given governing authority to the senior pastor, bishop and/or the apostle of that body of believers. They walk in the apostolic anointing to be responsible for and in charge of that local body of believers.

A common pitfall for prophets is mistaking their ability to hear and see prophetically as a license to not respect and submit to God's set authority in the house they are assigned to. In Numbers 12:1-11, the Bible records a situation where two prophets in the assembly of believers made this same mistake. Moses was the one God chose to lead His people. Moses had the authority and the assignment as the overseer of the congregation, just like a modern day pastor, bishop, apostle would today.

Miriam and Aaron were prophets that also were assigned to this same group of people. Because they had the ability to hear from God, the began to feel that they had the same position and rights to govern as Moses. They were familiar with Moses' humanity and imperfections and allowed that to cause them to not hold him in high regard.

*Then Miriam and Aaron spoke against Moses because of the Ethiopian woman whom he had married; for he had married an Ethiopian woman. So they said, "Has the Lord indeed spoken only through Moses? Has He not spoken through us also?" And the Lord heard it.*

**Number 12:1-2**

They did not understand the Biblical principle of submission to set authority. Oftentimes we feel that if we are to submit to someone's authority then that person must be greater than us, or better than us in our own evaluation. That would seem to be a logical conclusion to make.

However God's ways are above our ways and His thoughts are above our thoughts! The wisdom of God is foolishness to the carnal person. To have the mindset that a leader must qualify in our eyes in order for us to submit to them is a carnal one that is not led by the Holy Spirit.

Moses was not elected by a board of directors to be the leader chosen by God. Moses did not prove his qualifications to those who perceived themselves to be the leaders of the pack to convince them he was God's chosen. God Himself spoke for Moses and despite his inadequacies, inconsistencies and shortcomings, God established and set him as the leader or set authority of His people.

Many read this account of Aaron and Miriam's behavior and assume they were simply full of unfounded pride and rebellion. However to fully grasp this vital power principle, it is important to take a moment to reflect upon Moses' humanity and how their doubting of his authority was not unfounded or without natural reason.

Moses was raised in the Egyptian court of Pharoah as one of Pharoah's own children. This meant that while Miriam and Aaron knew that Moses was their blood brother, they also knew he was not raised in their important Hebrew way and customs. In our modern day, this would be the equivalent of Miriam and Aaron being "respectable" church going believers from their childhood while Moses was essentially raised in the world and not in church.

The Bible account also says that Moses was very humble, more than any other man on earth. We know that when Moses was called to lead God's people, he didn't feel he could possibly do it. He pleaded with God because he had a stuttering problem. God responded by telling him that he was going to appoint his brother Aaron to be his spokesperson.

So in the natural to Miriam and Aaron, Moses was raised in the world's ways and not God's ways. He was not versed in Godly traditions and ways of faith. In addition he didn't seem to have strong leadership skills as he was extremely humble which meant he would not be the kind of man who would carry himself with outward authority or put people in their place. In natural thought, many would consider someone with Moses' personality weak or lacking of a backbone.

As if that was not enough to make it difficult to submit to and respect Moses, it was also recorded that Moses didn't even know how to speak properly to people and needed Aaron to be his spokesman. So he's ignorant of their traditions and ways, he's a weak leader who doesn't stick up for himself, so much so that he stutters and cannot speak even for himself let alone for an entire group of people. To top it all off, he as now married an Ethiopian woman!

Hebrews aren't supposed to marry outside of their race and that was the final straw for Miriam and Aaron. They simply couldn't take it anymore. They come to the frustrated conclusion that Moses is not the only one who can hear from God. They were done submitting to him and they were now going to take their own authority in God's house.

This offended God so deeply that He appeared to them and dealt with it directly.   In this divine exchange, the Biblical principle of submission to authority for prophets in God's house was established and perfectly displayed.   God called the three of them out, Moses, Miriam and Aaron and He dealt with it.

*Then the Lord came down in the pillar of cloud and stood in the door of the tabernacle, and called Aaron and Miriam. And they both went forward. Then He said, "Hear now My words: If there is a PROPHET among you, I, the Lord , make Myself known to him in a vision; I speak to him in a dream. Not so with My servant Moses; He is faithful in all My house. I speak with him face to face, Even plainly, and not in dark sayings; And he sees the form of the Lord. Why then were you not afraid To speak against My servant Moses?" So the anger of the Lord was aroused against them, and He departed.*

**Numbers 12:5-9**

God takes respect for His set authority very seriously. Miriam and Aaron made the typical prophet's mistake. They thought that because they hear from God that it made them equal to or above the one God had chosen and placed in the position of what is now called apostolic anointing. Moses was a typology of the modern day senior pastor, bishop or apostle.

It is dangerous for you as a prophet to allow yourself to question or disrespect God's set men or women. As you grow in your office and gifting, you will also grow in the amount of influence you have and how many people follow you. The people will attempt to put you on a pedestal and cause you to feel exalted.

Because of this influence, God takes your attitude towards His authority structure very seriously. The most important thing to remember that submission to God's set leaders is not because they qualify in your eyes through their superiority or perfection. Your submission to His set leaders is the result of your heart focusing and trusting in His power and authority to hold your own life and the lives of those effected in His hands.

Apostolic leaders aren't chosen based on natural greatness, rather they are chosen based on God's specific assignment and perfect plan. His choosing is usually despite a number of shortcoming and unlikely leadership traits. Your submission therefore is your greatest act of faith through obedience to His plan and sovereignty.

Once you understand the ramifications of not being willing to submit and serve God's set leaders, it becomes a no brainer to make whatever adjustments are necessary to get on track with serving properly in God's house. There are many prophets who do not intend to be rebellious but who still end up causing some degree of confusion. This usually stems from a lack of understanding of the proper boundaries of their assignments.

The first step in understanding prophetic assignment boundaries in the local church is to understand the preeminence of the senior pastor's authority. He or she has the final responsibility to answer for the ministry operations and therefore he or she has the ultimate say in what will and will not happen there. No matter how stirred you are as a prophet, never step beyond the pastors instructions or trust.

God also establishes the scope of your assignment as a prophet by giving you specific instructions concerning the purpose of your operating as a prophet.

*"Pursue love, and desire spiritual gifts, but especially that you may prophesy... But he who prophesies speaks edification and exhortation and comfort to men."*

**1 Corinthians 14:1,3**

Your assignment as a prophet in God's house has a clear three fold definition. It is to speak edification, exhortation and comfort to men. The word "edification" is defined as the instruction or improvement of a person morally or intellectually. As a prophet this is a instruction that helps set a boundary. If anything you would say or do in God's house would cause you to not be edifying then you now know it is out of order for you to say or do whatever that is.

The word "exhortation" means to inspire and encourage. As a prophet in God's house this is yet another focus and boundary. All that you say and do should be inspirational and encouraging. It does not matter how others choose to conduct themselves. You must be like Joshua who declared "as for me and my house we will serve the Lord!"

The third focus for the prophet in God's house is to be a resource of God's comfort in times of challenging distress or frustrations. When people are going through distress and dealing with the hardships of life, receiving prophetic insight, wisdom and encouragement is a well spring of life. Knowing this is a function focus for the prophet in the local church gives the prophet direction and protection.

*Let two or three prophets speak, and let the others judge. And the spirits of the prophets are subject to the prophets. For God is not the author of confusion but of peace, as in all the churches of the saints.*

**1 Corinthians 14:29, 32-33**

It is clear that proper order and protocol are vital when it comes to how a prophet operates in the local church. The necessity of humility and submission to authority is profoundly important if the prophet is to carry the authentic signature of God. The source of confusion is not the Holy Spirit nor is anything that causes it inspired by God. God is a God of order and structure.

This order and structure is not meant to limit you in a negative way, but to give you guidelines to operate in. These guidelines allow the fullness of the flow of heaven to occur by protecting the environment from confusion, carnality and pride. It also provides safety and protection to you as God's prophet.

Also, the five fold ministry gifts are meant to work together in unity and harmony. Each one has its own assignment and some walk in multiple offices. However due to past abuses, some pastors and leaders are cautious or even resistant when it comes to working with prophets. While some may feel that this gives license for the prophet to disregard the convictions or hesitations of the pastors in order to "obey God" it actually is the exact opposite.

Because of God's design and desire for unity amongst the five fold offices, it is even more important that prophets regard and respect the set order of each local church. As more properly trained, properly submitted prophets emerge, repair of relationships between prophets and pastors will occur, unity will increase and the blessing will manifest even more in the body of Christ.

The office of the prophet is complex in its operations but it is functional within the order of the local church's protocol. The Apostolic (pastors, Bishops, Apostles) and the Prophetic ministry work together. In harmony they synergize the Body of Christ to fulfill the will of God. God has placed these gifts in the local church to function as a team for leadership and direction, which leads the church to righteousness. It is the prophetic anointing that has the eyes for a church to go and the apostolic anointing that understands how to get there.

# CHAPTER 9

## *THE SIGNATURE OF A SERVANT*

*Surely the Lord God does nothing, unless He reveals His secret to His SERVANTS the prophets.*

**Amos 3:7**

As we look into the story of Amos, we see his surprise of being ordained by God to be a prophet. He displayed humility and grace towards God for this calling. The heart that Amos displayed in his reaction to this calling speaks volumes.

In our time we see prophets with incredible gifts and powerful anointing to prophesy while lacking a spirit of servanthood and humility. Instead they become impressed with their own gifting and anointing and begin to display attitudes of superiority and self-importance. They come across as celebrities instead of servants.

There is a need to perform and put on a show coupled with a deep desire to be seen rather than heard. In my years of ministry I too have been guilty of this. It is important that we all understand that our Signature in the earth as a SERVANT will leave a far greater impact in God's Kingdom than being regarded as a celebrity or being seen as important and superior.

*Then Amos answered, and said to Amaziah: "I was no prophet, Nor was I a son of a prophet, But I was a sheepbreeder And a tender of sycamore fruit. Then the Lord took me as I followed the flock, And the Lord said to me, 'Go, prophesy to My people Israel.*

**Amos 7:14-15**

The attitude Amos displayed here is very profound. Amos was not schooled, taught, nor trained for ministry. He actually discovered that he was born to be a prophet while serving humbly as a sheep-breeder and farmer. It was Amos' simple obedience to God to hear Him and immediately obey Him that caused him to step into mass purpose and prophetic destiny. This is in direct contrast to some modern prophets who forget their humble beginnings.

When God starts revealing His secrets to prophets and as they begin to prophesy the heartbeat of God is when the true test of a prophet's character is revealed. Amos referred to God's prophets as

"SERVANTS." The definition of a servant is a person who performs duties for others, especially a person employed in a house on domestic duties as a personal attendant. Examples are a person employed in the service of a government, a devoted and helpful follower or supporter, or a tireless Servant of God.

As prophets we are here to execute governmental order from heaven to earth. We are employed by God. We take our orders from God and do nothing without God, who is the Commander and Chief, the supreme being on earth as well as heaven.

> *For I have not spoken on My own authority; but the Father who sent Me gave Me a command, what I should say and what I should speak.*

**John 12:49**

Even JESUS Himself didn't take the credit for the Words that He spoke. He is the Messiah and King and even He presented Himself as a servant. Just because you have a Word for someone or because you are constantly seeing visions or having divine insight into things, does

118

not always mean that you should speak and share what you see and know. A true servant of God only does what His Father specifically tells him to do. Servants are not presumptuous.

In order to leave your signature in the earth, you must be an example to the next generation that the most important characteristic of a prophet is that of a being servant. This is why so much of this book deals with the condition of your heart as God's prophet. Keeping your heart humble and submitted as a servant is a life or death situation for a prophet.

Having the heart of a servant must begin with prayer. The voice of God in His presence will always lead you to the right place spiritually, emotionally, mentally and physically. Therefore if you sacrifice your prayer time, you open yourself up to move out of the place of having a servants heart.

As servants it is also important that we stay in the stance of worship of the One who sent us. If we are constantly worshiping God and giving Him the honor and glory, it takes our focus off self and places it properly on Him. Worship causes us to stay connected to the reality that God is the only source of all we see, hear and know as His servants the prophets.

As prophetic servants, we are to be intercessors that stand for the needs and well being of others. It is not about us and our own needs. Our duty and assignment as His prophets is to stand in the gap and pray for people, communities, churches and nations. If we stay in this mode of assignment, we will not get entangled with our own needs, wants or desires. We know without doubt that we can trust God to keep us in every way because of this focus on His assignment.

Another key characteristic of a servant is to consistently walk in love and gentleness. This will keep you humble. Everything you do or say, even if it is a rebuke should be done in your love for God and your love for His people.

We must be gentle with people. I admit that I personally had to learn this the hard way. In my early days of ministry I was harsh, sounding like God was angry all the time and it made people feel like God was punishing them. I came to the realization that the reason for that was because I myself was prophesying from a hurting place.

It is important that as God elevates you in a position of serving His people, you must constantly deal with your own hurts and insecurities. If you do not deal with your internal insecurities, having an anointing and title will bring out the worst in you. You will subconsciously begin to feel your gift is for you to gain celebrity status and great wealth. If this happens, then you are headed for trouble.

Subconscious insecurities will cause you not to look at yourself as a servant but as a celebrity. Therefore, instead of having people be directed to God for ultimate help you will have them focus on you. You see this displayed when prophets feel that they are the only true prophet around and that people must look to them only for direction.

A insecure prophet's speech and mindset will often be focused on comparison. They compare themselves with others who are prophets and refer often to themselves as superior or senior. True servants do not compare themselves with others because they are too busy meeting needs of those they serve.

As prophetic servants, we are to be kind to people, not treating them as we are above them and talking down to them. People are attracted to your gift. However it is in displaying kindness toward them that they will respect you as well as the office that you walk in.

True servants display integrity, uprightness, honesty, wholeness, soundness, they do not envy nor display competitiveness. This is important as servants because God wants to trust you with being His mouth piece. You are representing Him and His kingdom. You cannot use your gift to manipulate people, to control them nor to sell out for money.

True servants are obedient and submitted to God. Even when we do not understand His ways, we must obey God. When an order is given, true servants do not question it, they simply obey. Jesus Christ our Lord and King always presented Himself as a servant.

Anytime we are at loss for how to conduct ourselves in any given situation to react like a servant, we can look to Jesus' perfect example. The old saying which sparked a rubber bracelet, bumper sticker and t-shirt trend was "WWJD?" There is so much power in pausing in our every day lives and stages of prophetic development and asking ourselves "what would JESUS do?"

*"Let this mind be in you which was also in Christ Jesus, who, being in the form of God, did not consider it robbery to be equal with God, but made Himself of no reputation, taking the form of a bondservant, and coming in the likeness of men. And being found in appearance as a man, He humbled Himself and became obedient to the point of death, even the death of the cross. Therefore God also has highly exalted Him and given Him the name which is above every name, that at the name of Jesus every knee should bow, of those in heaven, and of those on earth, and of those under the earth, and that every tongue should confess that Jesus Christ is Lord, to the glory of God the Father"*

**Philippians 2:5-11**

# APPENDIX
## *PROPHETIC VERSE CONCEPTS*

These Scripture references contain prophetic verse concepts that we've touched upon this book. They are meant for you to study and meditate on as you allow the Holy Spirit to continue to cultivate your signature as a prophet.

**2 Kings 17:13**

*Yet the Lord testified against Israel and against Judah, by all of His prophets, every seer, saying, "Turn from your evil ways, and keep My commandments and My statutes, according to all the law which I commanded your fathers, and which I sent to you by My servants the prophets."*

## Ezekiel 25:2

*"Son of man, set your face against the Ammonites, and prophesy against them.*

## Acts 3:18

*But those things which God foretold by the mouth of all His prophets, that the Christ would suffer, He has thus fulfilled.*

## Acts 11:27-29

*And in these days prophets came from Jerusalem to Antioch. Then one of them, named Agabus, stood up and showed by the Spirit that there was going to be a great famine throughout all the world, which also happened in the days of Claudius Caesar. Then the disciples, each according to his ability, determined to send relief to the brethren dwelling in Judea.*

## Acts 21:10-11

*And as we stayed many days, a certain prophet named Agabus came down from Judea. When he had come to us, he took Paul's belt, bound his own hands and feet, and said, "Thus says the Holy Spirit, 'So shall the Jews at Jerusalem bind the man who owns this belt, and deliver him into the hands of the Gentiles.'"*

## Numbers 12:6

*Then He said, "Hear now My words: If there is a prophet among you, I, the Lord , make Myself known to him in a vision; I speak to him in a dream.*